Prepping Without Paranoia

A checklist of things to take care of so catastrophe isn't catastrophe.

Author's note
This is a work of opinion. And no actions taken, or any consequences of said actions, as a result of reading this work are in any way the responsibility of the author, publisher, or distributor. By continuing to read this book you acknowledge that your choices are your own and the consequences of your choices, both good and bad, are also your own.

Table of Contents

Introduction

The ability to adapt, to pivot, to change strategy when life unexpectedly changes is the most valuable survival skill there is. Either we need to adapt quickly, or we need time to figure out a strategy. How quickly we can adapt, and how strategic we can be, depend entirely on the physical, mental, and relationship resources available to us. Likewise, how much time we have, to figure out how we are going to adapt depends on those same resources.

"Prepping" is just the deliberate creation and gathering of the resources that enable us to adapt quickly to any situation, or give us time to figure out how we should best react. And we already do this constantly. We put an umbrella in our vehicle on days it looks like it is going to rain, we keep a set of nice dishes to put on the table when important company comes for dinner, we program important phone numbers into our phones in case of emergency, we keep food in the freezer in case we can't get to the grocery store next week, we keep candles in the house in case the power goes out... constantly prepping!

By doing this we eliminate any fear associated with those situations. For example; Fear of the power going out is eliminated by having candles, food, and water stored. We know what we are going to do if the power goes out, so we stop being afraid of the situation.

There is nothing fancy about this short book. It gives some direction about where to think, and what to acquire to protect yourself, and your family in a catastrophe. Whether that catastrophe is natural disaster, contagion, financial collapse, civil unrest, drought, war, alien invasion, or anything else... It is about becoming less and less reliant on institutions and systems set up for you... and more reliant on the systems you set up for yourself! Giving you the greatest ability to adapt to any situation, and eliminate any paranoia about those situations.

Some of these steps are generic and will need to be adapted to your own situation. Every family's finances, location, circumstances, and comfort level are different. And you will need to *adapt* what you find here for yourself. Other steps are quite specific, but even then, you will need to weigh what you learn here to meet your own family's needs and wants. In no way is every step perfect for every person. But it will change how you think. Give you direction if you want it. Get you started with ideas of how to prepare, or add ideas to help you with what you already have prepared.

If, while you go through this, you think of things that are not in this book... then add them to your own preparations. If you disagree with anything, then *adapt* the thought processes to best help you and your situation!

Step 1: The Mind

The first level of a prepared person is the mind! We must think differently and have access to multiple levels of thought about all situations. Since most of us have never experienced hardship on a level that forced us to just barely survive... we have a difficult time imagining all the circumstances we might encounter.

But we can read to stimulate the imagination. Sometimes this involves reading things that we wouldn't normally, or that we find hard to stomach. This pushes the mind into thinking outside of our normal box. Reading also builds reservoirs of knowledge in our mind. Answers to questions that may come up... and solutions to situations we would not normally find ourselves in!

Novel Recommendations
-One Second After by William R Forstchen
-Island in the Sea of Time by SM Stirling
-The Skystone by Jack Whyte (book 1)
-The Singing Sword by Jack Whyte (book 2)
Resource Book Recommendations
-150 Healthiest Foods on Earth by Johnny Bowden
-Fear, Duty, or Purpose by Brad Harmsworth
-What Would The Rockefellers Do by Garrett Gunderson
-True Wealth Formula by Hans Johnson
-10 Packs for Survival by Joel Skousen
-The Prepper's Blueprint by Tess Pennington
-Strategic Relocation by Joel Skousen
-The High Security Shelter by Joel Skousen
-The Secure Home by Joel Skousen

Own the physical books! All the resources we can read are useless to us if we lose access to electricity, or the internet.

Step 2: Get Healthy

Good health is the foundation for surviving almost any situation. Our minds need to remain cool and methodical. Terror, and panic are a death sentence when catastrophe is upon us. If our physical bodies can react and adapt to any situation, it will allow our minds to do so as well.

-Eliminate addictions and other reliances: Drugs, alcohol, caffeine, medications, sugar, pornography, etc... every place we are addicted is a place we may be forced to go through withdrawal. Not usually at a convenient moment. Every place we are reliant on someone else to function everyday (ie. Medications, vision correction, etc.) is a place where we could be forced to act when maybe it isn't the safest to do so.

-Drink clean water: The water that most of us drink every day is filled with toxins and elements that our body must filter out while trying to keep us hydrated... Filter your water. Our top recommendation is that your home owns a *Berkey water filter* and uses it every day.

-Read; *150 Healthiest Foods on Earth*. And let it modify how you eat and grocery shop.

-Start Taking Vitamins: We can no longer get everything we need from our food because of the farming practices of our modern world. We need to take supplements to get the vitamins and minerals that enable our bodies to be healthy.

If you don't already have vitamins you like, our top recommendation is *Pure*. (www.livepure.com/wc) They have a liquid multivitamin and a Sulphur product that everyone should take every day!

-Plant a Garden and start eating your own produce!

-Maintain a Physical Fitness routine: Something (or more than one thing) that builds both physical strength and increases Physical stamina. Martial arts, bodybuilding, running, even walking everyday if that is all you can do!

-Get out in Nature: Have regular time in nature without "man-made" interference. Leave the phone behind and spend time in the park, or at the beach. It resets the mind and increases vitality.

Step 3: Get Wealthy

While wealth is not the answer to everything, in most situations it gives us more options. And almost all the steps on this list require at least a little wealth... some steps require a lot.

-Get out of Debt! Being owned by a lender or a bank is a place where you can be controlled... controlled people build wealth with difficulty.

-develop a wealth plan: Get the *Wealthbuilder app*, sign up and learn those systems inside out and backwards. Or book a consultation with *Watchman Consulting* (You can do so through their Facebook page, or their website) they have an excellent system designed to integrate different incomes and focus money easily towards goals.

-Read; *What Would the Rockefellers Do*
-Read; *True Wealth Formula*

-Use properly set-up life insurance policies to secure wealth both for yourself, and for your children.

-Start a Business: Learn how to be a producer, instead of a consumer. This teaches valuable skills that are useful in any economy. It also allows you to build wealth when most others are unable to.

Step 4a: Fill your Safe

In time of crisis we must be able to purchase what we need, and protect what we have. History shows us, repeatedly, that governments eventually take away the people's ability to do both of these things. History also shows us that without these abilities... people do not survive very long during catastrophe.

The Bank has legal right to limit how much we can withdraw. They can also stop us from withdrawing anything at all! As well under certain circumstances, the government has legal right to confiscate physical gold and silver bullion owned, and kept, by you. These have been done many times in history.
What they do not have the right to confiscate from us is cash! So we can do two things:

1. Keep $5000-$10,000 cash outside of the bank: Somewhere we can get to it. Preferably a safe in our home, but a safe in a storage locker will also work, or with someone we trust. Just not in a bank account or Safety Deposit Box.

2. Keep $5000-$10,000 in silver coins. But very specific types of silver coins. They <u>must have a monetary value stamped on them</u>. This way they are "usable as cash" and are more difficult to confiscate.

Our Recommended choices are;
-*"Junk silver"*: These are actual coins from history, dimes, nickels, and quarters, that have a high percentage silver content.
-The *Canadian Maple leaf:* It is the most recognizable bullion in the world, and has $5 stamped on it.
-The *American Silver Eagle:* It is highly recognizable, one of the most beautiful, and has $1 stamped on it.

Step 4b: Fill your Safe

Governments have historically confiscated firearms in times of crisis. They know where many of them are from "Registration programs" and they take them away right before, or during, the most dangerous moments in history.

-Read; *Fear, Duty, or Purpose* and let it modify how you think about protection

-Take some shooting classes and train yourself how to shoot well, how to carry a firearm, and how to move when you shoot.

-Own one handgun per responsible person in the home. (9mm or .22)

-own at least 2 rifles (.22 and .308, or .22 and .556) or shotguns (12guage)

-2000-10,000 rounds of each caliber ammunition

-2-6 aerosol cans of defense spray (OC or red pepper)

Step 5: Store Water & Food

In every crisis there is always the first "storm". The first weeks where catastrophe happens. That catastrophe could be weather related, or disease related, civil unrest, war, terrorism, economic collapse, alien invasion... it doesn't matter. Most people have only a few days of food and water in their home, and when it is gone, they must go out looking for more. Into the middle of the ongoing "storm" where it is unsafe. Having enough food and water to get you through this first period of time is essential... having enough to get you longer is even better.

Water

-Purchase a *Berkey water filter*!!! It will allow you to have clean water no matter what!!! As long as there is a source of water, no matter how dirty, you can filter it clean for years without replacing any parts.

Food

You can find lists by other experts (read: *10 Packs for Survival & The Prepper's Blueprint*) of how much of every food type to store... but in this age where time is so valuable, I recommend you use a little wealth, and buy someone else's product for your long-term storage food.

Other than long term food storage, the food we store must be something we eat already!!! So that we can cycle it and not let it go bad in a sort of "rolling storage system". For example: Peanut butter, Always keep an extra jar of peanut butter in the pantry... when you finish the jar you are currently using, you take the second jar out of the pantry and you replace it immediately with one you purchase! This way there is always food stored in case of emergency.

-Have 3mo-1yr of food stored for your entire family. Long term storage food is the easiest. *watchmansupply.com* has some recommended brands, both organic and non-organic, that will ship both 3-month and 1-year kits to your door.

Extra "everyday use" recommended foods to supplement your long-term food
-Peanut butter (Very calory dense, important for quick energy)
-Your *Pure* vitamins
-Vitamin C!!!!
-Oats
-Chia Seed
-Cooking oil
-Salt
-Honey (will never go bad)
-Eggs (chickens if possible)
-Frozen meat (May need generator to keep freezer cold. recommend a Solar generator, or quiet Honda generator)
-Dehydrated food
-Canned food (will need a hand operated can opener)
-Spices and dry condiments to make food more exciting Especially Cayenne pepper (it can be used to sterilize wounds and stop light bleeding – painful but effective)
-Powdered Milk (or if you can have goats for fresh, do that)
-Garlic and ginger, and more garlic
-Baking ingredients like Flour, Sugar and Salt… what would you need to bake bread?

Cooking and eating
Hot food is something that boosts morale hugely, and allows us to consume many more options. Also allows us to sterilize water and food that might be "iffy"

-Propane stove or grill
-Propane, Lots of it (Propane will never go bad)
-Firepit and firewood
-Fire starting medium (matches, lighters, lighter fluid)
-Cast iron cookware (it can be used on any heat source, even put directly into a fire)
-Wooden cooking utensils (make less noise on iron cookware than metal utensils do)
-Paper dishes for eating (if water is hard to get, washing dishes is tough)

Extended eating
To do this long term you want enough food to keep you until you have other food options available.
-Plant a garden, or store a *seed vault* of heirloom seeds so you can start one
-Gardening tools
-Gardening books
-Fishing/hunting skills & equipment

Step 6: Store the Necessities

Use the same system as the food... a rolling storage system. Keep extra and cycle it into use when you finish something. Always replacing the extra IMMEDIATELY.

-Toilet paper and paper towels

-Hygiene items (toothbrushes and toothpaste, hand soap, shampoo, tampons, etc...)

-LIGHT (so important!!! Candles, lanterns, batteries for flashlights or reading lamps, solar chargers for rechargeable batteries, etc...)

-Sanitation (Lots of garbage bags, Ziploc bags, dawn blue dish soap, disinfectant liquids (Lysol, isopropyl alcohol, thieves, Everclear alcohol, bleach, etc...)

-Entertainment (board games, card games, puzzle books, reading material, etc...)

-Tools (basic hand tools, plumbing tools, woodworking tools, gardening tools, nails and screws, axe and saw, etc...)

-Clothing (both warm weather, and cold weather)

-Medical (Personal medications, Large generic first-aid kit, gloves, Trauma First aid kit, rubbing alcohol, Silver gel and spray, Tylenol/Advil, eye-drops, lip balm, swabs and pads, Benadryl and EpiPen, caffeine pills (for headaches), scalpel, sutures, burn gel, Aloe Vera (or an Aloe plant), etc....)

-Baby items (diapers and wipes)

-WARMTH (so important!!! Blankets, firewood, heating fuel, wood-stove, propane heater, etc...)

-Multi function items like Everclear Alcohol, Pink Solution, Cayenne pepper, Honey, Baking Soda, and Charcoal

-Items for barter (coffee, cigarettes, alcohol, and ammunition will most likely be the most valuable. But think "what will people in my area need?" food, clean water, light... all the things you need.)

-Seeds for your garden (long term storage, heirloom seeds)

Step 7: Build Community

This needs to happen constantly and is not really step 7... but works throughout everything.

We cannot survive alone. Not as an individual, and not as an individual family! We must have allies and people we can trust. So be a trustworthy person, and constantly make friends! Watch for people who think similarly to your own family, who also look to the future as something to prepare for, and not something to just allow to happen.

Society teaches that we are stronger alone, this is a lie. In the survival world the first thought is that we need more resources to provide for more people... this is true. But with more people there are also more hands to help acquire resources, and less worries.

If there are people to protect and take care of the children, then others have less fear over their safety and can focus on other tasks. Maybe it is working in the garden, or going out to trade for supplies, or hunting through abandoned homes for anything useful... We can't do everything needed in a disaster on our own!!!

More people = more skills = more capability = more protection = more rest, etc...

Build strategic relationships with people whom you can trust. And deliberately learn skills that will benefit the community you have built.

Step 8: Build a "Go-Bag"

If you had 10min to get out of your house, what would you need? What would you need to survive for 3-7 days? What would you need to survive, and travel cross country for 3-7 days? This is the purpose of the go-bag. It has everything you need to survive to get to your next safe place.

-there must be a go-bag for each person in the home, including children and babies.
-it must suit your environment. Urban environments require different equipment/supplies than wilderness environments do
-it needs to be kept up constantly, cold weather supplies/equipment changed for warm weather, and vice versa, when the seasons change
-there should be a bag in each vehicle, for the purpose of getting you home if something happens while you are out

You can build your own with these principles: Protection, protection, protection.
-Protection from the elements: What will I need to keep the weather from harming me? Clothing, shelter, a heat source
-Protection from starvation/dehydration: What will I eat, and how will I get clean water? Water filter, food to eat
-Protection from living creatures: if things are really bad, what will I need to protect myself and my supplies from others? A way to hide what I have, or perhaps defend it.

If you don't want to build your own, you can find suppliers who build them for you. *www.watchmansupply.com* currently is our top choice. They have both complete bags, or checklists so you can build your own. A good Go-bag is not usually cheap ($2000-$5000), but it will give you far more options in time of crisis than if you don't have one.

Step 9: Have a Getaway Vehicle

If we have enough warning, and we live in a potentially unsafe area, we should be leaving immediately. A tougher, reliable vehicle that you can just throw your belongings into and drive to a safer place (maybe an ally's home) is a good thing to have.

Important requirements of your getaway vehicle:
-all weather, all terrain capable
-Older, preferably carburetor-controlled and not fuel-injected
-With Trailer Hitch, locking gas cap, heavy duty tires
-Great choices include *4Runner, Suburban (Chevy or GMC), Old Land Rovers, Land Cruiser, older Jeeps*
-2-wheel option for taking off into the bush: *Rokon* is our top recommendation

Important things to have stocked in your getaway vehicle:
-Car care items (oil, coolant, fuses, tire pressure gauge, tire pump, fix-a-flat, jack, spare wheel or tire, tool kit, knife, jumper cables)
-Ammunition for the firearm you carry, and the one in your go bag
-Rotary hand pump, bolt-cutters, and hacksaw for when fuel is not available for purchase
-Mask and gloves in case of medical or viral emergency
-flashlight and blanket
-water filter or filter bottle
-Food bars
-Also, if you can find one, get an extra ignition computer. Wrap it in a towel and keep it in a metal box (like an ammo can)

Step 10: Buy or Build a Secure Home

The largest step in preparing for catastrophe is to purchase or build a safe place to go. If family or friends have a farm away from major population centers and transportation routes... what can be built or set up there? If your Health and Wealth steps have been successful you may want to move to a small community, or acquire a hobby farm out in the country, or a cabin in the wilderness. If you have enough wealth, I recommend you build a secure home. An innocent-looking home that does not stand out as being anything special but is designed to protect your family and allies from whatever happens.

Any secure home you build should have:
-Distance from population centers and transportation routes
-A water source that is exclusively yours, a well, stream, or lake
-Hidden rooms
-Walls that are bulletproof
-Minimal Heat and Air Conditioning requirements
-Alternate heating capability like a wood-stove or wood-fired furnace
-Outdoor cooking facilities
-A garden and greenhouse
-Alternate energy options like a generator, or solar power
-A secure garage
-Alternate toilet facilities like a composting toilet or deeply dug outhouse
-Alternate fuel sources like large Propane stores, or wooded areas for firewood

Conclusion

When catastrophe occurs, in whatever form that is, how much time will you have to adapt? Which items from the checklist on the next pages do you already have? And which do you still need?

The more prepared you are for any catastrophe, the less fear there will be! Use the steps in this book, and the checklist in the back, to give your family time!!! Making sure there is no fear or paranoia before anything bad happens... or in the middle of a catastrophe itself.

Lots of these materials, supplies, ideas, and systems are available from many places. Build your own, or look around to get good prices, and work with people you trust. *Watchman Consulting*, and *watchmansupply.com* exist to try and provide the pieces, or council, for every step in this paper. From providing clean water, to teaching how to build legacy relationships, to designing secure homes... but the most important thing is that your family is protected no matter what happens. That you have the knowledge and the materials to survive any, and every, disaster or catastrophe that will happen in your family's life.

Checklist

Books

- O   One Second After
- O   Island in the Sea of Time
- O   The Skystone
- O   The Singing Sword
- O   150 Healthiest Foods on Earth
- O   Fear, Duty, or Purpose
- O   True Wealth Formula
- O   What Would the Rockefellers Do
- O   10 Packs for Survival
- O   The Preppers Blueprint
- O   Strategic Relocation
- O   The High Security Shelter
- O   The Secure Home

Health

- O   Berkey
- O   Vitamins
- O   Garden
- O   Workout Routine

Wealth

- ○ Wealth Builder App
- ○ Life Insurance Policies
- ○ Start Business

Safe

- ○ Cash
- ○ Silver
- ○ Handguns
- ○ Rifles
- ○ Ammunition
- ○ Pepper Spray

Food

- ○ 3-month food supply
- ○ 1-year food supply
- ○ Peanut Butter
- ○ Vitamin C
- ○ Oats
- ○ Chia Seed
- ○ Oil
- ○ Salt

- O Honey
- O Eggs
- O Meat
- O Dehydrated\canned food
- O Spices
- O Powdered Milk
- O Garlic/Ginger
- O Baking ingredients
- O Propane stove/grill
- O Propane
- O More Propane
- O Firewood
- O Fire starters
- O Cast Iron Cookware
- O Wooden Cooking Utensils
- O Paper Dishes
- O Seed Vault
- O Gardening Tools
- O Gardening Books
- O Fishing/hunting gear

Necessities

- Toilet paper/paper towels
- Toothbrushes/toothpaste
- Hand soap
- Shampoo/conditioner
- Tampons
- Candles
- Lanterns
- Flashlights/batteries
- Battery charger
- Garbage bags
- Ziplock bags
- Dawn Blue Dish Soap
- Disinfectant liquids
- Board games/card games
- Books
- Hand tools
- Plumbing tools
- Woodworking tools
- Nails/screws

- O   Warm weather clothing

- O   Cold weather clothing

- O   Medications

- O   General First-Aid kit

- O   Trauma First-Aid kit

- O   Nitrile gloves

- O   Rubbing Alcohol

- O   Colloidal Silver gel/spray

- O   Tylenol/Advil

- O   Eye drops

- O   Lip balm

- O   Swabs/pads

- O   Benadryl/EpiPen

- O   Caffeine Pills

- O   Scalpel & Sutures

- O   Burn Gel

- O   Aloe Vera

- O   Diapers/wipes

- O   Blankets

- O   Heating fuel

O Woodstove

O Propane heater

O Everclear Alcohol

O Cayenne Pepper

O Baking Soda

O Charcoal

O Barter items

Go Bags

O Go-Bags for home

O Go bags for vehicle

Vehicle

O Tough/Reliable Vehicle

O Engine oil

O Coolant

O Tire pressure gauge

O Fuses

O Tire pump/fix-a-flat

O Jack/Spare wheel or tire

O Car tool kit

O Jumper Cables

- ○ Rotary Hand Pump
- ○ Bolt Cutters
- ○ Mask/Gloves
- ○ Flashlight
- ○ Blanket
- ○ Water filter
- ○ Food Bars
- ○ Ignition Computer

Home

- ○ Secure Home

Enjoy this Book???
Many items referenced here can be found at
www.watchmansupply.com

Including Brad Harmsworth's other Book

26